HUMOR ME
I'm Over the Hill

Barbara Johnson
HUMOR ME
I'm Over the Hill

THOMAS NELSON
Since 1798

NASHVILLE   DALLAS   MEXICO CITY   RIO DE JANEIRO   BEIJING

Published in Nashville, Tennessee. Thomas Nelson is a tredemark of Thomas Nelson, Inc.

Thomas Nelson, Inc. titles may be purchased in bulk for educational, business, fundraising, or sales promotional use. For information, please email SpecialMarkets@ThomasNelson.com.

Unless otherwise indicated, Scripture quotations used in this book are from The Holy Bible, New International Version (NIV). Copyright © 1973, 1978, 1984, International Bible Society. Used by permission of Zondervan Bible Publishers.

Other Scripture quotations are from these sources:

The Holy Bible, New Century Version (NCV), copyright © 1987, 1988, 1991 by Word Publishing, Dallas, Texas 75234. Used by permission.

The Living Bible (TLB), copyright © 1971 by Tyndale House Publishers, Wheaton, Ill. Used by permission.

The Message (MSG), copyright © 1993. Used by permission of NavPress Publishing Group.

Many of the stories, jokes, and quips included in this volume have been contributed to the author as unidentified clippings or Internet postings, and although diligent attempts have been made to identify the material's origin, in many cases this was impossible. When these items are specified as "source unknown," the author claims no rights or ownership. Selected items in *Humor Me, I'm Over the Hill* have previously appeared in the author's earlier books published by Word Publishing and W Publishing Group. While the author's personal experiences related here are true, details may have been changed to protect identities or exaggerated to accommodate the author's great love of laughter. Some anecdotes are composites of the author's or her acquaintances' experiences or products of their imaginations.

Library of Congress Cataloging-in-Publication Data
Johnson, Barbara (Barbara E.)
    Humor me, I'm over the hill / Barbara Johnson.
       p. cm.
    ISBN 10: 0-8499-0289-4 (hardcover)
    ISBN 13: 978-0-8499-0289-5 (hardcover)
    1. Life—Humor. 2. Aging—Humor. 3. Women--Religious life. I. Title.
BD435.J64 2007
305.26'20207—dc22

                                                      2007003159

Printed in the United States of America
07 08 09 10 11 WOR 9 8 7 6 5 4 3 2 1

Dedicated to

my fellow adventurers in aging

CONTENTS

NOT THE WAY I PLANNED IT

I'm ready to meet my Maker . . .
but He's apparently tied up with a previous engagement

If you know anything about me, you're aware that I attract strange and funny incidents the way refrigerators attract magnets. Now that I'm teetering on the tightrope between *senior* and *senility*, these things seem to be happening more frequently. For instance, during the week before my birthday last December, my phone rang, and the conversation went something like this:

"Mrs. Johnson?"

"Yes."

"This is Fred from Real-Life Prostheses, and . . ."

"Excuse me? Who is this again?"

"Fred, from Real-Life . . ."

"I think you have the wrong number, Fred."

"I just wanted to let you know that your new breasts aren't ready yet."

"My new what?"

"Your husband called and asked us if we could do a rush job and have your new breasts ready before Christmas. The other guy told him yes and promised to have them ready tomorrow, but then we realized you were an extra-large, and since that takes longer, they have to be special ordered. I didn't know the other guy told your husband yes; he shouldn't have done that without checking with me. I'm so sorry."

I've had occasional memory lapses lately, so I took a quick glance down at my chest to make sure nothing was missing.

"Fred, I . . ."

"Oh dear. He probably wanted it to be a surprise. He said you were going somewhere special for Christmas, and he knew you would want to look your best."

"Fred, I'm so sorry to argue with you, but I really don't think my husband called you. He died three years ago, and I just checked—yes, I still have my own breasts. And by the way, they're not what you would call extra—"

"Oh, my! Oh, dear! I am *so* sorry. I can't imagine how this happened. I . . . well . . . I. Uh, have a nice day."

See how good God is? On any given day, He might have a stranger call you up unexpectedly and give you a laugh that lasts for weeks, if not for a lifetime. So the laughter lasts longer—and may reoccur sporadically as you share the story with friends. That's what happened when I told my pals about the phone call . . . and the next week, when they showed up with my birthday cake, it was shaped like, well, let's just say it was anatomically correct . . . or at least anatomically suggestive!

Hunting Down the Humor

When you get to be my age—and if you're reading this book, you're probably headed that direction—you've probably had lots of opportunities to laugh at life's silliness. Of course, sometimes the stuff that happens to us as we move through the maturity maze doesn't seem all that funny at the time. Sometimes you have to hunt down the humor, pick it out of the problem pileup, or crank it up from the cesspool. But if you look hard enough and live long enough, you'll find it. As Carol Burnett reportedly said, "Humor is tragedy plus time." And if you're extra lucky, over the decades you've developed just the *slightest* gift for exaggeration, so that when you tell your friends about funny things that God has sent your way, you find yourself improving on the humor of God Himself.

On the other hand, things that used to be funny when I was younger aren't all that hilarious anymore. For instance, my sister, Janet, used to play the piano at a nursing home to entertain the residents, and we loved to laugh together about the optimistic old lady who bragged to Janet, "I wake up every morning and I know who I am, and I say, 'Praise the Lord!'"

Yes, that *used* to be funny. These days, however, it's losing a bit of its punch. Oh, I know who *I* am most of the time. It's *your* name I can't remember. Sometimes I'll have to run through my entire mental Rolodex, calling a friend by every name that comes to mind—from former pets and automobiles to present-day helpers and relatives—before I finally arrive at the right one.

Now, I have to admit this isn't really a *new* problem. I can remember how our boys used to roll their eyes as I was reciting roll call, trying to get to the right name for the culprit who needed an emergency lecture: "Bill! Steven! Whumphie! Tim! Barney! Spot! David! . . . You there, chasing your brother with the scissors! Stop it right now!"

As I've grown older, the problem has gotten worse, especially with all the abbreviations and acronyms used in modern life. Lately I've sometimes felt like an English teacher who's struggling to make sense of a foreign alphabet. I might mean to report on a friend's female problems requiring hormone replacement therapy that worried her about someday needing life-saving intervention but instead say that she had frequent parcel deliveries along with worries about the war in Iraq and hoped she would never need an accountant. So it comes out as, "She had such bad UPS, she thought she needed to take WMD but worried it might affect her heart and cause her to need CPA."

I'd like to blame my tendency toward confused communication on the fact that—maybe you've heard—I was diagnosed with a malignant brain tumor back in 2001. But the fact is, I've always been just a little bit absentminded, so I'm not sure the brain tumor has anything to do with it. (When the doctor told me what the problem was, I thought, *Wouldn't you know? All these years I've wished my brain would GROW and instead I get a GROWTH!*)

For me, having brain cancer has been one long headache. People treat you differently when they find out you have cancer, especially people who are acquaintances rather than close friends. They look at you differently, and a lot of the time, I don't like the unspoken words I see in their eyes: *Poor you. You've got cancer. You're going to die.*

It's made me want to follow another cancer patient's urges and wear a T-shirt that says:

Yes, I have cancer.
Yes, I'm going to die.
And so are you.

Cancer has taken away my freedom to travel and my ability to work as a conference speaker, which I've enjoyed for more than thirty years. I admit that I've shed many tears about my situation. Yes, indeed. I've endured *plenty* of anguish during the last half decade, which has sent me crying to God, complaining about the way He was bringing my life to a close.

But then . . . unexpectedly . . . I kept on living! Imagine that. I've spent my life looking forward to heaven, and just when I thought I had caught a glimpse of the pearly gates, what do you know? God wasn't ready for me yet. Either that or, as the old saying goes, the more you complain, the longer He lets you live.

So I've vowed to stop complaining (or at least try to stop). Instead, I hope to follow that old maxim that says,

Live each day as though it's your last . . .
and someday you'll be right!

My Goal: Giving You a Giggle

So, whenever I can manage it, I dry my tears, blow my nose, and find something to do—and especially, some-

"You are what you eat. If you want to reach a
ripe old age, eat a lot of brown bananas."

thing to laugh about. I can no longer travel to huge are-
nas around the country, sharing my story and relishing
the sound of the audience's laughter ringing in my ears,
but I can try my best to give you a giggle or two by sharing the funny stuff friends, family, and readers still send
me every day in the mail. And I can ridicule the silly
moments I've experienced on my way to senior citi-
zenry—like the phone call from the breast-maker man
and the resulting anatomically correct birthday cake.

The best laughter, of course, is the kind that's shared.
As I've put this little book together with the help of a
couple of friends, I've imagined you joining in with us
as we have chuckled our way through the assorted stories, jokes, cartoons, and calamities we've compiled in
these pages. We've tried hard to find where all these

little jewels of joy came from, but where no source is given, we do not know it.

For me, one of the funniest things about this volume is that, if I'm not mistaken, it is my *fourth* "last book" since the brain tumor was diagnosed. Everyone, myself included, assumed I'd soon be moving on to heaven, and my friends at W Publishing Group—my longtime publisher—wanted to send me off with glorious fanfare, so they encouraged me to write about my hilarious (and heart-wrenching) brain-tumor experiences. That book, published in 2002, was *Plant a Geranium in Your Cranium.*

We all waited awhile, and nothing happened. Well, all sorts of things *happened*, but none of them ushered me into eternity, so in 2003 we did another book, *Humor Me: The Geranium Lady's Funny Little Book of Big Laughs.*

In 2004, because I'd already hung around Earth way longer than anyone expected, we confidently put together *Laughter from Heaven*, sure that when it landed in readers' hands it would seem like a little gift of glorious giggles fanned down by me from heaven, where I was happily waving my angel wings.

Apparently there was a waiting list for wings.

I decided since I wasn't moving on to perpetual retirement, I might as well get back to work, so last year's book was *Humor Me, I'm Your Mother*, a collection of funny stuff for anyone who is a mother—or *has* a mother.

*"I'm fifty-seven years old, but with the wind-chill
factor I feel eighty-three."*

Frankly, it's a little embarrassing, after all these enthusiastic farewells, to still be down here gathering goofy
stuff when I thought I'd be singing with the saints by
now. But here it is 2007, and I'm still living, still laughing,
and still growing older, so once again, I'm loading up
another book with lots of laughter and sending it out to
you, hoping it will encourage you to search out all the

fun and joy hidden in each new day God grants you on our beautiful—and boundlessly funny—Planet Earth. I don't know about you, but I now plan to live happily to be one hundred—or die trying!

OVER THE HILL HEARTWARMERS

I'm not old.
I'm chronologically gifted.

♥

Lynda came to have lunch the other day in the assisted-living facility where I've been living lately. As we were sipping our soup, a bald-headed man, one of the residents, walked by and said, "Boy, you girls are lookin' good today. You're the youngest-looking ones here!"

My friend smiled coyly and sat up a little straighter, enjoying the man's attention.

But I'd heard it all before. I rolled my eyes and said, "Don't pay any attention to him. He's ninety-two; *everyone* looks young to him!"

Lynda laughingly shared the story with her long-time friend, Jan, who's been single for a while. She listened to Lynda's description and said, "Well, clean him up and send him on over!"

—BJ

♥

CLOSE TO **HOME** JOHN McPHERSON

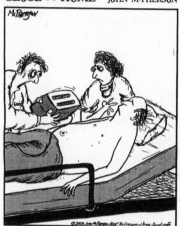

"Our defibrillator paddles are broken!
Stick his hands in this toaster!"

♥

I don't really care if my hearing's going. The only
thing people say to me anymore is, "Have you
taken your medicine?"

—GENE PERRET[1]

♥

By the time you find greener pastures . . .
you can't climb the fence!

♥

When you get to be my age, you're well acquainted with pain.

The challenge—and for me it's a big one—is not to *be* a pain to others.

♥

Some days you're the banana. Other days you're the blender.

Some days you're the bug. Other days you're the windshield.

Some days you're the pigeon. Other days you're the statue.

Some days you're the dog. Other days you're the fire hydrant.

Some days you're the salmon. Other days you've got salmonella.

Some day you're the colonoscopy technician. Other days you're the . . .

No, let's not go there.

—BJ

♥

I'm not old.
I'm just overdue for eternity.

♥

Even to your old age and gray hairs I am he, I am he who will sustain you. I have made you and I will carry you; I will sustain you and I will rescue you. (Isaiah 46:4)

FINDING NEW PURPOSES IN LATER LIFE

How to use age spots, skin tags, and facial hair to camouflage those extra chins

Don't bother me with the facts. In my opinion, *menopause, hot flashes, mood swings,* and *chin hair* are *all* four-letter words. And frankly, they're all proof, to me at least, that God is indeed male.

Sure, it was a good idea to design women so that their reproductive abilities taper off as old age approaches. I've said for years that the reason women over fifty don't have babies (or at least they didn't *used* to have babies) is that we'd lay 'em down somewhere and forget where we put 'em. Most women accept this fact as a sound decision on God's part. As we age, we have enough worries wondering if we'll soon be living in a world of our own drool and diapers; we don't need the added stress of dealing with someone else's.

It's true. We twenty-first-century retirees are a wonderfully busy bunch and have an amazing assortment of activities that keep our minds working and our bodies moving. For instance, we can spend all morning trying to remember why we've just walked into the bedroom carrying a can of oven cleaner. Or we may become valuable members of our community's crime-stoppers program as we cruise the neighborhood for hours trying to remember why we're in our cars and where we were going when we left home.

"If we take a late retirement and an early death, we'll just squeak by."

Differences in Aging

Just examine the differences in how God sends men and women through their midlife crises. Aging men tend to focus on one dominant emotion during this stage: fun. They buy themselves red convertibles; show up poolside wearing plaid shorts, flowered tank tops, and black socks; decide to take up disco dancing; and suddenly become self-appointed experts on everything, expounding endlessly on topics ranging from home decorating to global warming.

Women, on the other hand, are swept through this stage by hormonal hurricanes that may *start* with fun (single-handedly consuming a gallon of mocha-praline-apricot swirl, for example, on our way to have our corns removed at the podiatrist's office). But inevitably each episode ends in anguish (perhaps prompted by our spouses making some outrageous comment such as, "What's for dinner?").

Personally, I remember menopause as a mainly *moist* stage of my life. The dampness could be prompted by things that once might have seemed trivial but during this stage became tremendous. When I wasn't wiping away tears during crying spells brought on by the latest heartbreaking incident (Bill's forgetfulness about putting the seat down on the commode, for instance, or the failure of the glue to hold down the envelope flap when I was paying the light bill), I was sopping up sweat generated by progressively powerful hot flashes.

Menopause is a time of mystery as well as moisture, and it's also an indication that God is not only male but also a comedian. The first mystery may be why that hormonal highway of emotions has such incongruous detours. We're floating along on a tidal wave of sorrow because the dryer lint won't come out of the filter in one piece, and the next thing we know, a family member calls hello as he walks by the laundry room, and we angrily reenact an interrogation right out of *Law and Order*: "What's *that* supposed to mean? Where were *you* when your socks had to be sorted?"

And then there are those hairy issues involving hair. This is the part that assures us God is a comedian. At the same time over-the-hill men are consumed with worrying about the departure of hair from their heads and its sudden, overly enthusiastic sprouting from nostrils and ear canals like a bumper crop growing in a Kansas wheat field, menopausal women are stunned to find the stuff appearing in places on their bodies where it never had the nerve to show up before. While men are dialing up the infomercials' phone numbers to order follicle stimulants, scalp massagers, and "lifelike" toupees, we're trying to decide whether to have our new chin hair bleached, waxed, lasered, or permed. You just have to wonder sometimes: *what were You thinking, Lord?*

And here's another mystery. Why, just when we finally have time to relax in our Barcaloungers and eat bonbons nonstop all day long, do we end up with bodies that need—how can this be?—*fewer* calories and *more* exercise!

I heard one guy say he thought his weight had increased due to all the kidney stones he carried around. But his wife quickly added that the weight of the stones had to be more than offset by his increasingly obvious reserves of natural gas.

"Ewe again?"

By the time you get to be my age—and especially if you're struggling with the health problems I've endured—you start to put weight and fitness issues behind you. Maybe that's what prompted one jokester to note that old age brings us the wisdom to accept the fact that life sometimes throws us curves—and we're sitting on our biggest one. This is probably the same wise person who observed that we take on deeper thoughts and become more reflective during our golden years, pondering the bigger issues of our existence, including such questions as, "What is the meaning of life?" and "How much Healthy Choice ice cream can I eat before it's no longer a healthy choice?"

"Can't quite make it out, Mrs. Gurnbach? And we drove here all by ourselves, did we?"

Because of the brain tumor, as well as other problems that have affected my eyes, my vision isn't nearly as good as it used to be. And as difficult as it's been to accept that handicap, it's also been a blessing. You see, when I look in the mirror these days, I'm not quite as sharp as I once was (in more ways than one). The image I see reflected there is just a bit blurry, which allows me to fill in the details with my imagination. And what do you know? My imagination sees the Geranium Lady as she was in about 1975. I love it! In my new mirror image, I'm tall, thin, and perfectly coiffed. And best of all, I only have one chin!

(Now, to be honest, I may be smoothing over a few of the 1975 Geranium Lady's minor flaws, not to mention ignoring the fact that she wasn't "born" until 1990, when my book *Stick a Geranium in Your Hat and Be Happy* was published, but you'll just have to trust me on this: these days in my mirror, she looks great!)

The whole point of this chapter focusing on over-the-hill health and beauty (and I *do* have a point, even if it takes me awhile to get to it), is to remind you that the way we think about ourselves greatly influences the way we "see" ourselves. For me, that used to be a cliché. Now it's a fact.

For all I know, I may have grown an extra nose and have elongated earlobes that swing in the breeze. (Just kidding. I'm not blind, just borderline bananas. I can see well enough to know I haven't evolved into a one-eyed alien, at least not yet.) While my eyes are preoccupied with problems, my heart has been given *new* eyes that see me the way God sees me. And girlfriend, let me tell you, in His eyes, I'm lookin' good!

Transformed Inwardly by an Outward Focus

The title of this chapter talks about finding new purposes in life as we age. Although the subtitle jokes about finding new purposes in beauty tips (at least I didn't indulge in that well-known pointer that suggests using hemorrhoid ointment as a wrinkle reducer), the fact is that finding new meaning in life, whatever stage we're in, can transform us into beautiful people. One of the ways we do that is by reaching out to help others, even when we find ourselves in a difficult situation.

My pal Lynda shared with me a story about that kind of inspiring person. She found it in Robert Morgan's book *Then Sings My Soul: 150 of the World's Greatest Hymns*, in the story about the origin of the hymn "God Leads Us Along."

The Youngs spent their lives in service to God, traveling around the country leading church revivals. They were poor, surviving on donations, but they finally managed to save enough to have a small home of their own. While they were away on a preaching trip, an arsonist burned the house to the ground, and the Youngs lost everything except what they had carried with them on their trip. It was that loss which inspired George Young to write the beautiful lyrics of the hymn, including this inspiring chorus:

God leads His dear children along.
Some through the waters, some through the flood,
Some through the fire, but all through the blood;
Some through great sorrow, but God gives a song,
In the night season, and all the day long.

Years later, an admirer of the Youngs set out to find them. By then George had died, and the friend was shocked to find Mrs. Young living in a ramshackle county poorhouse. He expressed great sorrow at her situation, but she wouldn't hear of it, insisting that she was right where God had led her.

"Sorry . . . got a frog in my throat."

©2007 Casey Shaw.

She explained that aging, destitute people were continually moving into the poorhouse to live out the rest of their lives, and many of them arrived in a hopeless, faithless state of abject misery. "I'm having the time of my life introducing them to Jesus!" Mrs. Young said. "Isn't it wonderful how God leads?"[1]

Let God lead you into a beautiful new stage of life by showing you the plans He intends for you: "plans to prosper you and not to harm you, plans to give you hope and a future," no matter how many farewell tours you've completed and no matter how many "last books" you've written![2]

OVER THE HILL HEARTWARMERS

I've taken up swing dancing.
Not on purpose. Some parts of my body are just prone to swinging.

♥

We all get heavier as we get older . . . because we have a lot more information in our heads.

♥

A woman went to the doctor's office, where she was seen by one of the new doctors. But after only a few minutes in the exam room, she burst through the door, screaming as she ran down the hall.

An older doctor stopped her and asked what the problem was. She told him her story, and after listening, he had her relax in another room while he investigated.

The older doctor marched down the hall to find

the first doctor. "What's the matter with you?" he barked. "Mrs. Smith is sixty-three years old, has four grown children and seven grandchildren, and you just told her she was pregnant?"

The new doctor continued to write on his clipboard and without looking up said, "Does she still have the hiccups?"

—SOURCE UNKNOWN

♥

©2007 Barbara Johnson.

♥

When we women hit middle age, we start wishing for something that will hide our wrinkles. A beard is the last thing on our minds.

—MARTHA BOLTON[3]

♥

Sigh spotted at an optometrist's office: If you don't see what you're looking for, you've come to the right place.

♥

Over the years, I've learned who is my friend and who is NOT my friend. *Gravity* is NOT my friend!

♥

Here's one way to eliminate sagging skin: eat 'til the wrinkles fill out!

♥

Gray hair [is] the splendor of the old. (Proverbs 20:29)

Chapter 3

THE LOVELY PATINA OF AGE

*Of course I'll smile for the camera . . .
just as soon as I find my teeth*

A couple of years ago, after enduring many months of chemotherapy and other cancer treatment, I fell and broke *both* arms. The medications had apparently made my bones brittle, and since Bill was in the last stages of his own short, vicious battle with bone cancer, there was no way I could stay at home while I recuperated. I needed full-time care, and he was too weak and sick to help me—in fact, at that time hospice nurses were coming in each day to help *him*. So I had no choice but to stay in a skilled nursing facility for several weeks.

It was a miserable move. I hated leaving Bill, hated

leaving my home, and to make matters worse, the facility's orthopedic rooms were all occupied, so at first they put me in a completely different area. I was so frustrated by it all that when Lynda came to visit, I nearly bit her head off. "I can't stand it here!" I told her. "You've got to get me out of here."

"Barb, what's wrong? Why are you so upset?" Lynda asked, alarmed by my screeching voice and wild eyes.

"Can't you tell?" I hissed at her. "This is the looney bin! It's where they put people with . . . oh, shoot . . . the ones with . . . oh, for cryin' out loud. What *do* you call that disease where you can't remember anything?"

With that, Lynda burst out in hysterical giggles—which didn't help my mood one bit.

"What *are* you laughing at?" I fumed. "If you think it's so funny, *you* move in here, and I'll go home. Here. Just help me get my clothes on, and I'm outta here."

"Oh, Barb," Lynda said. "Don't you see how funny that is? There's no room for you in orthopedics, so they've put you in the Alzheimer's unit—but you *can't remember* what it's called!"

"Lynda, that is NOT funny!" I scolded. "And I most certainly *can* remember that it's called the Alzheimer's unit. I was trying to think of that other word, the, uh, scientific word, you know, the one the *professionals* use."

"Oh. Right. Sorry, Barb," Lynda said, trying hard to stifle the next wave of giggles threatening to erupt.

I've had a hard time since then convincing my family and friends that I have *not* lost my mind . . . or my memory. But they keep bringing it up . . . and, I guess, since I'm telling you the story now, I might as well join them in the laughter.

The midlife woman's biological clock

The Fun of Forgetfulness

The incident, and the resulting laughter it has generated (*now*—it wasn't so funny at the time), helps me introduce the idea that, well, forgetfulness can be fun. It can also be frustrating, of course, especially for those people who have to listen to us tell the same story we've forgotten we already told them a dozen times. So let's just acknowledge the cold, hard facts: the older we get, the more we tend to repeat ourselves.

Also, the older we get, the more we tend to repeat ourselves.

And maybe you've noticed that, sometimes, diehard members of the over-the-hill gang have nothing interesting to say . . . and can't stop talking about it. Really. It's enough to make the rest of us nod off in total distraction. (Well, OK. I admit it: some of us have a special knack for nodding off anytime and anyplace, whether we're focused *or* distracted.) As someone pointed out, as we get older, our stories get longer.

One of the things I find most irritating about my own increasingly frequent memory failures is not just forgetting facts and thoughts but also forgetting where I put things. You've heard the adage that the journey of a thousand miles begins with a single step. Well, for me, any journey to anywhere always began with one last trip to the bathroom and a frantic search for my car keys.

I'm amazed at how those ornery things simply disappeared. One minute I was holding them in my hand—and the next they'd vanished into thin air. A few hours later, I might find them hiding in the vegetable bin of the refrigerator or nestled between the pillowcases in the linen closet. If I didn't know better, I'd think the place was haunted by a pesky pack rat.

And I know I'm not alone in experiencing these frustrations over lost things and forgotten facts. One of my friends says she spends most of her time "searching for

Minnie Pauz.....™   by Dee Adams

© www.minniepauz.com

The mystery of the missing household and personal items becomes painfully clear!

a little piece of paper with some extremely crucial number written on it." Phone numbers, addresses, lock combinations, passwords, appointments, birthdays, and even Social Security numbers—all things involving numerals seem to share that special talent for vanishing, either from sight or from memory.

More and more, as I experience this disappearing-number syndrome, I empathize with that sweet little old lady who was asked by an interviewer how old she was. The woman stared off into space, trying to find the answer in the recesses of her memory. Finally she said, "Do you need to know right now, or could you wait awhile?"

The Persistent Problem of the Purse

The most amazing thing we women lose—at all stages and all ages of our lives—is our purse (often with our car keys in it). We've all done it: set it on top of the car while we're loading groceries at the supermarket, put it down on a changing-room chair while we're trying on clothes in the mall, left it in the taxicab, forgotten it on an airplane, walked out of a restaurant while it remains under the table, overlooked it as we hurried out of the doctor's office when we were late picking up our kids from school.

Yes, we forget our purses, lose our handbags, misplace our wallets, and leave our pocketbooks behind. But how can that be? We might as well leave our brains behind (which, for some of us, also happens) as leave these little (or not so little) envelopers of essentials. Our whole *lives* are contained in those things! Driver's license, credit cards, keys, address books, membership cards, family photos, cameras, cell phones, calculators, garage-door openers, dental floss, cosmetics, mirror, hairbrush . . . oh, and occasionally, money. With so much of our lives stuffed in there, it seems impossible that we could ever walk off and forget it. But we do.

One of my friends has packed her big purse so full of absolutely essential items that she's barely able to lift it anymore. So she leaves it behind in the car. She calls her big purse "the mother ship" and carries only a smaller clutchpurse (the "satellite") with her. It's a strange system, but she insists she's able to function better, knowing the rest of her absolutely essential stuff isn't too far away.

I once wondered aloud how men could exist with only a set of small pants pockets. "I'll tell you how they exist," a woman answered loudly. "They make *us* carry all their stuff around." And with that, she opened her cavernous bag and started pulling out all her husband's absolutely essential stuff: sunglasses, eye drops, nose spray, passport, airline tickets, chewing gum, wadded-up restaurant receipts, and a three-hundred-page paperback.

And while we somehow manage to walk off and forget our essential-packed purses occasionally, it's always been interesting to me to think back on what and where I was when I realized my purse had gone missing. More than once I've been standing in the grocery-store checkout lane, my cart piled high, when I realized I had no way to pay for the mountain of items I'd hoped to buy. (And incidentally, like that unknown quipster, I've noticed that these days about half the stuff in my cart says, "For fast relief.")

Yes, in many homes, the three little words that are heard most often are not "I love you" but "Where's my purse?"

One friend told me that right before her aging mother-in-law went around the mental bend into la-la land, she left her handbag somewhere, and the family never did find it. But the sweet old gal had never left home without it for seventy-some years, so whenever the family prepared to go somewhere, most often a doctor's appointment, this high-decibel conversation usually echoed through the house:

GROWN DAUGHTER, CALLING FROM THE FRONT DOOR OF THE HOUSE: "Mom, let's go. We're late!"

MOM, YELLING FROM BACK IN THE BEDROOM: "I'm coming. I just need to find my purse."

DAUGHTER: "You don't need your purse. I've got your Medicare and insurance cards."

MOM: "Don't be silly. I *do* need my purse. I just put a new package of Gas-X in there."

The sounds of drawers opening and closing and doors slamming are heard. The voice escalates.

DAUGHTER: "MOM, seriously. Just come on. I've got everything you need."

MOM: "I know it's here somewhere."

DAUGHTER: "MOM, YOU LOST YOUR PURSE BACK IN FEBRUARY!"

MOM: "Don't be ridiculous. I didn't lose my purse. I had it just a few minutes ago . . ."

Mom, a widow, was at the stage where she really needed others to care for her, so her daughters had all her important cards and papers replaced and kept them in their own purses. Still, it became so difficult to get Mom out of the house without her purse that the family bought her a new handbag just like the old one she had lost. They filled an old wallet with family pictures and a few dollar bills, added some tissues and a new package of Gas-X, and hid it in top of the hall closet. Then, when the inevitable search for the purse began before every departure, one of the kids could say, "I've got your purse, Mom," and hold it up for her to see.

This solved many of the problems but not all of them. Mom had always been most generous in picking up the check whenever she and her family went out to eat. During these later, forgetful years, she would pick up her new purse from under her restaurant chair, discreetly fumble around inside looking for her money or her credit card, and then loudly proclaim for all the other diners to hear, "I'VE BEEN ROBBED!"

Senior Shenanigans

Adult children and caregivers have to be ingenious to cope with their forgetful parents and other family members. I hope I never put my friends and relatives through the shenanigans I've heard about from others, but I also know that once we begin that plunge over the hill, we have little control over whether we slide into total dementia—or take a delightful stroll through the golden years. If we end up in la-la land, all we can do is hope our loved ones have lots of patience . . . and a strong sense of humor.

"No, dear. The phone's working fine — you just answered the TV remote."

© 2003 Barbara Johnson

It's a common thing for those suffering from Alzheimer's or other memory problems to become paranoid, believing, like the old lady who lost her purse, that others—generally the ones trying hardest to help them—are up to no good. One woman was nearly driven insane herself by her elderly mother's continual phone calls accusing her of such mischief as moving her furniture, stealing her favorite clock, and hiding bananas in the fingers of her garden gloves.

This is the same dear mother who bought herself the very best dentures money could buy. It took several dental appointments to remove her old teeth and get the new dentures fitted. Her daughter dropped Mom off at her home the day she got her beautiful new smile . . . and none of the family ever saw those dentures again. Mom insisted someone had come in during the night and stolen them.

Yes, these incidents are hilarious . . . when they're not happening to *us*. Until they do, let's just keep on laughing . . . and praying! God has promised us He will give us the strength we need to get through whatever comes our way. And as we head out over the hill, His Word guides us in preparing for the bumps we'll inevitably hit along the way.

A friend put together this beautiful little collection of reminders about how God wants us to live. She knew that an alphabetical list would be much easier for us over-the-hill folks to remember:

The **A** **B** **C**s of Godliness

Acknowledge Him. **B**e kind. **C**all to God. **D**o good. **E**ncourage one another. **F**orgive. **G**ive generously. **H**umble yourselves. **I**nvite the poor. **J**udge not. **K**eep yourself pure. **L**ove your neighbor. **M**ind your own business. **N**ever forget His precepts. **O**bey God. **P**ray continually. **Q**uench not the Spirit. **R**ejoice. **S**ing praises. **T**rust Him. **U**nderstand the Lord's will. **V**isit the fatherless. **W**alk humbly with God. E**X**amine your ways. **Y**ield to Him. **Z**ip your mouth.

A—Proverbs 3:6; **B**—Ephesians 4:32; **C**—Psalm 55:16; **D**—Luke 6:27; **E**—Hebrews 3:28; **F**—Ephesians 4:32; **G**—Romans 12:8; **H**—1 Peter 5:6; **I**—Luke 14:13; **J**—Matthew 7:1; **K**—1 Timothy 5:22; **L**—Matthew 19:19; **M**—1 Thessalonians 4:11; **N**—Psalm 119:93; **O**—Acts 5:29; **P**—1 Thessalonians 5:17; **Q**—Hebrews 11:34; **R**—Psalm 118:24; **S**—Psalm 47:6; **T**—Psalm 3:5; **U**—Ephesians 5:17; **V**—James 1:27; **W**—Micah 6:8; **X**—Lamentations 3:40; **Y**—Romans 6:13; **Z**—Psalm 39:1.
(Compiled by Betty Bunfill, Gainesville, MO, © 2007.)

OVER THE HILL HEARTWARMERS

Life is not meant to be easy, my child;
but take courage: it can be delightful.
—GEORGE BERNARD SHAW

♥

I have what every man who has that many
candles on his birthday cake needs around him—
a large group of friends and a working sprinkler
system.

—RONALD REAGAN[1]

♥

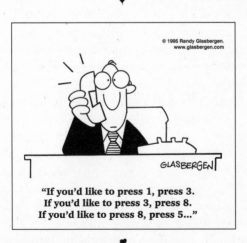

© 1995 Randy Glasbergen.
www.glasbergen.com

GLASBERGEN

"If you'd like to press 1, press 3.
If you'd like to press 3, press 8.
If you'd like to press 8, press 5..."

♥

Funny, I don't remember being absentminded.

♥

Thank you for calling the Senility Hotline.

If you've forgotten why you called, please hang up and call again later.

If you think you've called before but can't remember, please hang up, wait for the dial tone, then press the redial button on your phone. If we answer, this is not your first time.

If you *think* you called but can't find the redial button, please hang up and find someone who can read the buttons to you.

If you know you've called before but *still* can't remember why you are calling, press 7, and someone who's also clueless will come on the line to chat about the time the woman in front of you in the grocery-store line snagged her pantyhose on the candy rack and pulled down the whole display, including magazines and breath mints, before you could get your cart out of the way.

If you're wondering why *we* called *you*, we're sorry to break it to you . . . we know you're a really nice person and all . . . , but no, we didn't.

If you've lost your glasses, trust us: you've probably dialed the wrong number.

If you're calling for help with incontinence issues, please hold.[2]

♥

In *The Importance of Being Earnest*, Oscar Wilde wrote, "Memory . . . is the diary that we all carry about with us." Which explains why, the older we get, the harder it is to remember anything. Our diaries have gotten too big to lift!

♥

"As I get older, I find I rely more and more on these sticky notes to remind me."

♥

I have a memory like an elephant. In fact, elephants often consult me.

—NOEL COWARD

♥

My, how we've changed:
Then: long hair
Now: longing for hair

Then: Rolling Stones
Now: kidney stones

Then: hoping for a BMW
Now: hoping for a BM

—SOURCE UNKNOWN

♥

A conclusion is the place where you got tired of thinking.

—STEVEN WRIGHT

♥

Jesus said, ". . . I tell you the truth, when you were younger you dressed yourself and went where you wanted; but when you are old you will stretch out your hands, and someone else will dress you and lead you where you do not want to go." (John 21:18)

Chapter 4

CELEBRATING SENILITY

All the smart and good-looking seniors are relocating
to Looneyville . . . I'm just writing to give you my new address

After all those books and all those years of making
wisecracks about tottering off to the Home for the
Bewildered, guess where I've ended up. Well, techni-
cally I'm still a few jokes away from being truly bewildered, but I do reside now in an assisted-living facility.

Frankly, it's not *living* I need assistance with. It's
walking. Also dancing, skipping, jumping, playing hop-
scotch, and bouncing on the backyard trampoline to do
my rapture practice. Judging by the tumbles I've taken
in the last year, I've still got what it takes for somersaults
and pratfalls, and despite the tumor, my brain seems to

be bopping along pretty close to normal (well, not that it was ever *too* close to normal). The problem is that my everyday mobility has become a challenge.

And even *that* wouldn't be so bad, except that I *forget* that I'm not as agile as I used to be. So, for instance, if the phone rings while I'm in the bathroom brushing my teeth, I tend to turn too quickly and set off at a gallop for the telephone table like I've done for thousands of years (or at least a few decades). And suddenly I once again find out the hard way that my racing days are apparently over and what I'm actually doing is *rolling* for the telephone instead of running.

"Who gets Meals on Wheels?"

So here I am, temporarily away from home. But I'm still busy, and I'm still working, with the help of my son, to keep up with Spatula Ministries, the outreach organization Bill and I started thirty years ago to help peel parents off the ceiling with a spatula of love when they've landed there due to some problem with—or the death of—their children. We started Spatula, hoping to provide help and encouragement to families who were going through some kind of hurtful experience. Having lived through the death of two sons and the homosexuality of a third, we wanted to help other parents avoid the mistakes, heartache, and alienation we had endured—and learn to laugh again.

That ministry continues with the help of my friends and my son David, who has stepped in to help me handle the mail and the ministry's newsletter and outreach efforts. What a blessing he has been! He's even putting together a Web site for me (www.Barbara SpatulaJohnson.com).

Now, to be honest, it's unlikely that I'll ever become computer savvy enough to operate the Web site myself. But we knew the Internet would be a good way for me to keep my Spatula families updated and help them connect with each other. David has promised to print out the messages you leave for me on the site, so it's *almost* like I'm sitting there at the computer screen. And it gives me that little extra touch of sophistication, so valuable here in my home away from home, where I love to impress my new friends with casual references to my Web site, as though I actually know what I'm talking about.

High-Tech Failures

My *old* friends, on the other hand, aren't so easily impressed. They know I have trouble operating a door-bell, let alone an electronic device, and they're quick to remind me of past experiences when I've endured funny failures during attempts to move into the high-tech era.

"The ringing in your ears—I think I can help."

For example, there was the time Bill talked me into getting rid of my four IBM Selectric typewriters and replacing them with a new word processor. (We had four Selectrics because, knowing I *loved* typing on them, whenever any of our friends moved on to computers they offered me their old Selectrics, and I happily accepted. The late Erma Bombeck also had four Selectrics, so I like to think I was just joining her in her writing method.)

The electric typewriters had begun to show their age, and Bill was tired of hauling one after the other to the repair shop to have them fixed. So he finally convinced me to try a new word processor—an electronic machine with a memory and other amazing features. Word processors were supposedly much simpler to operate than a real computer but still one step closer to letting me think of myself as high tech.

The momentous morning arrived when Bill loaded the typewriters into his car and disappeared out of the neighborhood. Filled with excitement (along with just a tiny morsel of apprehension), I watched him go and then faxed my friend this note:

THIS IS A NEW DAY! Today Bill is taking my FOUR IBM Selectrics to a guy and has ordered me a brand-new different kind—with a memory or something. I am saying good-bye to the machines that have typed all my books and newsletters for 20 years!!!!!!!! How I will miss them. But he is tired of taking them to be fixed. So the next you hear from me will be on a BRAND-NEW lovely machine, which I will have to learn how to operate.

The reason I know what I wrote that day—March 10, 2000—is because my friend, knowing me all too well, *kept* the fax so we could laugh about it later. That time came the very next day, when I sent Bill packing off the "brand-new lovely machine" with orders not to come back until he had bought back my Selectrics from the typewriter shop! That day was my first and last foray into the modern age of computers. But it was just the beginning of another reason for laughing with my friends—and that made the whole frustrating experience worth the hassle.

Earthly Energizers

My friends are such a treasure to me, a true gift from God, especially in my present situation. During these last few years, through all the heartache and headaches I've endured, they've been the earthly energizer that has kept me going. They cried with me when cancer struck and grieved with me when Bill died. And they've treated me to more trips to Marie Callender's for "emergency pie therapy" than I can begin to count.

With David's help, they hosted a book-signing event for me here in my temporary home, and they surprised me with that custom-built birthday cake I mentioned at the beginning of the book. Most importantly, they've encouraged me to cling to God for strength as strongly as I cling to them for friendship. By keeping *their* focus on God's gracious goodness and the strength of His everlasting arms, they inspire me to keep *my* face turned toward Him as well.

And they keep me laughing. Just last week my pal Lynda called and said this year she was reading *The Message* Bible all the way through and she had come upon a verse that made her think of me. "Oh, Barb, God gave me the *best* verse for *you*. I read it and thought, *I've* got *to share this with Barb*."

"That's great, Lynda," I said. "What's the verse?" I heard the sound of pages fluttering and the *clunk* and *thunk* of various things falling to the floor.

"Oh! I dropped it," came the muffled sound from the other end of the phone line. "Let's see . . . it was . . ." More pages were turned. "Well, Barb, I've lost it. Oh! There it is. No, that's not it. Maybe it was . . ."

"Well, the Lord giveth, and the Lord taketh away," I said.

"I'll call you back, Barb," Lynda said. "I'm sure He'll give it to me again."

Someone said that a truly happy person is one who can enjoy the scenery on a detour. Well, I'm on a detour right now, and friends like Lynda keep me laughing during the delay. This isn't the route I'd planned to take on my way to eternity. I wanted to stay busy and active, traveling all over the country to spread my joy right up until I took my last breath.

But it seems God has other plans for my departure from earth, so I'm doing my best to "enjoy the scenery" while I'm traveling this detour on the way to heaven, knowing that, however it comes, my final exit here will be my grandest entrance *there*.

OVER THE HILL HEARTWARMERS

Let us endeavor so to live that when we come to die even the undertake will be sorry.

—MARK TWAIN

♥

Advice for the aged: If at first you *do* succeed . . . try not to look surprised.

♥

How far you go in life depends on your being tender with the young, compassionate with the aged, sympathetic with the striving, and tolerant of the weak and the strong—because someday in life you will be all of these.

—GEORGE WASHINGTON CARVER

♥

A dinner speaker was in such a hurry to get to his engagement that when he arrived and sat down at the head table, he suddenly realized that he had forgotten his dentures.

Turning to the man next to him, he said, "Oh dear, I forgot my teeth."

The man said, "No problem." With that he reached into his pocket and pulled out a pair of dentures. "Try these," he said. The speaker tried them. "Too loose," he said.

The man then said, "I have another pair—try these."

The speaker tried them and responded, "Too tight."

The man said, "I have one more pair. Here—try them."

The speaker said, "They fit perfectly!" With that he ate his meal and gave his address.

After the dinner meeting ended, the speaker said to the man who had helped him, "Thank you for coming to my aid. Where's your office? I've been looking for a good dentist."

The man smiled and answered, "Oh, I'm not a dentist. I'm the local undertaker."[1]

♥

God made us sisters.
Prozac made us friends.

♥

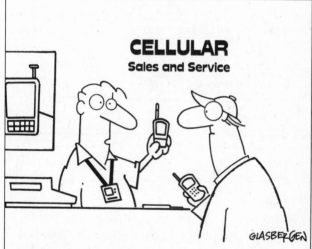

"Nothing is 'just a phone' anymore. On this one, the antenna doubles as a nose-hair trimmer!"

♥

During a visit to the mental asylum, a visitor asked the hospital's director what the criterion was that defined whether a patient should be institutionalized.

"Well," said the director, "we fill a bathtub with water, then we offer a teaspoon, a teacup, and a bucket and ask the patient to empty the bathtub."

"Oh, I understand," said the visitor. "A normal person would use the bucket because it's bigger than the spoon or the teacup."

"No," said the director. "A normal person would pull the plug."

—SOURCE UNKNOWN

♥

♥

Joy is not in things; it is in us.

—RICHARD WAGNER

♥

Friends love through all kinds of weather, and families stick together in all kinds of trouble. (Proverbs 17:17 MSG)

MOTHERING MIDLIFE MAYHEM

Are you sure you're the person I gave birth to?

Someone once said that no matter how old her children get, a mother is constantly watching for signs of improvement. I could be the poster child for that sentiment. My two surviving sons have grown into handsome, talented, and smart young men. Oh, wait. They've suddenly become middle-aged men, I guess. But I have to admit that, as much as I love them and as much as I love them and as much as they mean to me, I still worry about them.

And I know I'm not alone. I have a friend in the publishing business who spends a lot of time at her computer, both at work and at home. She has two adult children who revel in the busy, independent lives they enjoy in other parts of the country while remaining closely tied to Mom's apron strings . . . or maybe I should say, to her computer cable. The problem, this mom admits, is that she has spoiled her grown children, not financially or materially, but through her computer skills.

I'll call this mom Pam, although that isn't her name. (She says if I use her real name and her children can be identified, they would probably never get a job anywhere, should they actually manage to wrap up their many years of college and decide to apply for one someday.) The situation is a real Catch-22, because the problem stems from her closeness to her children, which the mom is grateful for. But, as many of us know, there are some things parents would rather *not* know about their kids' activities.

Exciting Conversations

For Pam, the six most dreaded words her kids can say to her from their cell phones are, "Mom, are you at your computer?" You see, if they call and ask this question, it usually means they're lost—who knows where?—and are hoping she'll go online to help them find themselves. For example, Pam's daughter once called from a taxicab in the Midwest:

DAUGHTER: Mom, are you at your computer?

Pam (bracing herself): Where are you?

Daughter: Who would have thought a cabdriver wouldn't take a credit card? Can you go online and find an ATM in downtown St. Louis?

A few years ago in February, this phone call came from Pam's son:

Son: Mom, are you at your computer?

Pam (fumbling with the phone in the dark): Tom, it's four forty-five in the morning. Why would I be at my computer?

Son: Oh, just wondering . . .

Pam: Where are you?

Son: Listen, Mom. I don't have time to talk. Could you just look online and get me directions to the Fleabag Hotel . . .

Pam: *Hotel?*

Son: In New Orleans?

Pam: NEW ORLEANS! WHY WOULD YOU NEED DIRECTIONS TO A HOTEL IN NEW ORLEANS?

Son: Mom, relax! We have reservations.

Pam: Tom, it's Thursday. Aren't you supposed to be in *Houston*? You know, where you go to college?

Son: My roommate and I were studying last night, you know, and we realized it's almost time for Mardi Gras. So we decided to hop in the car and drive to New Orleans. Don't worry, Mom. We brought our books;

we're gonna study. We just forgot to bring the printout of how to get to our hotel. So could you just look it up for us? We're almost there.

Now, I have to admit that Pam's experiences are completely foreign to me because, as I mentioned, my sons are more likely to call me and ask, "Mom, are you on Mars?" than, "Are you on your computer?" But I've had my own share of strange, terrifying, and even heartbreaking phone calls from and about my sons. And over the years I've also worked with thousands of parents who've endured equally distressing phone calls or bad news delivered in other ways. On the one hand, we want to know the truth—and on the other, well, sometimes we'd rather have surgery without anesthetic than hear:

"Mom and Dad, I'm gay."

"I have AIDS."

"I'm on drugs."

"I'm so sorry, Mr. and Mrs. Smith, your son . . . I'm *so* sorry—"

Those of us who've survived *real* heartbreaking pronouncements like these can't help but laugh now at the things that *used* to send us into orbit:

"Sorry. I can't talk now. I just got my tongue pierced."

"I'm getting an F in English."

"I dented the fender."

"I lost your credit card."

"I burned the cake and destroyed the kitchen, but the rest of the house is still standing."

"I'm moving out."

"I'm moving back home."

Yes, as bad as they were at the time, those once-disastrous statements seem pretty tame to us now. Of course, we're different people today than we were back then—older and (we hope) wiser, among other things. As someone said, children can be a blessing to us in our old age, but they can sure help us get there faster too! And when we do, we may start agreeing with that other jokester who said, "Today is the tomorrow you worried about yesterday . . . but not nearly enough!"

"I don't care if she is a tape dispenser. I love her."

Bonding Lessons

One thing that happens to us as we get older is that, even though our childbearing years may be behind us, many of us find that our families are still expanding— with in-laws and grandchildren.

Most of us probably try to be on our best behavior around our children's in-laws and prospective in-laws, especially during the get-acquainted stage (knowing we shouldn't misbehave or embarrass the ones who will be helping our kids pick out a nursing home for us some- day). One of my friends, Laura, a single mom, shared a funny story about her misdeeds and miscues as she was getting acquainted with her daughter's fiancé, Rob.

When Laura's daughter Renee announced their engagement, Laura was acquainted with Rob but didn't feel she really knew him. So she arranged some little get-togethers at various times in different settings so the three of them could visit and "bond," as Laura said. Of course she wanted to make a good impression on Rob, for her sake as well as for Renee's.

Still, the Saturday morning they agreed to meet at a little coffee shop for breakfast came at the end of a very tiring workweek. After such a hard week, "my feet wanted, and in my opinion, deserved, to feel loved," Laura said. "So I allowed them to wear their softest bright pink fuzzy slippers into the restaurant."

Of course Renee was mortified that her mother would wear bedroom slippers to a restaurant, and she didn't hesitate to tell her mother so! As Laura and Renee went back and forth, discussing what Renee insisted was her mother's poor fashion sense, "Rob just listened quietly as I defended my feet for their choice of shoes," Laura said.

About a week later, the three of them planned another outing, this time to have dinner at a casual Mexican restaurant, complete with mariachi band. "After dinner, Renee and Rob left together to continue their date, and I went home," Laura said.

The next morning Renee told her mother that Rob had been especially quiet on the way home. When Renee asked what was wrong, "he told her that he was expecting me to wear my slippers and I hadn't, and that neither of us had even noticed that he had worn *his* slippers so I wouldn't feel uncomfortable," Laura said.

Talk about bonding! "No one has ever cared about my feet so much," Laura said.

She's now totally delighted with her daughter's husband-to-be, and when she thinks about it, she says, it should really come as no surprise to her because, even though she didn't meet him until just recently, "I have been praying for him since the day Renee was born!"

I hope you'll pull on *your* fuzzy slippers and join me

now in some ridiculously revitalizing humor for us over-the-hill parents.

OVER THE HILL HEARTWARMERS

One day a father was talking to a friend about his son, who had caused great heartache. The friend said, "If he were my son, I would kick him out."

The father thought for a moment then said, "Yes, if he were your son, so would I. But he is not your son; he is mine, and I can't do it."

—SOURCE UNKNOWN

♥

"For Pete's sake, Dad! It's just a worm. Let him have it."

♥

God is too good to be unkind, and He is too wise to be mistaken. And when we cannot trace His hand, we must trust His heart.

—Charles Haddon Spurgeon

♥

Little kids' answers to important questions:

Q. Why did your mom marry your dad?

A. My dad makes the best spaghetti in the world. And my mom eats a lot.

Q. Who's the boss at your house?

A. Mom doesn't want to be boss, but she has to because Dad's such a goofball.

Q. If you could change one thing about your mom, what would it be?

A. I'd make her smarter. Then she would know it was my sister who did it and not me.

—Source Unknown

♥

They say when you die there's a light at the end of the tunnel. When my father dies, he'll see the light, make his way toward it, and then flip it off to save electricity.

—Harland Williams[1]

♥

A doting father used to sing his little children to sleep . . . until he overheard the four-year-old tell the three-year-old, "If you pretend you're asleep, he stops."[2]

♥

I never know what to get my father for his birthday. I gave him a hundred dollars and said, "Buy yourself something that will make your life easier." So he went out and bought a present for my mother.

—RITA RUDNER[3]

♥

Then you will call out, and the LORD *will answer. You will cry out, and he will say, "Here I am." (Isaiah 58:9 NCV)*

Chapter 6

GROW OLD ALONG WITH ME

We started out with nothing
and still have most of it left

Someone sent me a funny story about a woman's husband who had been slipping in and out of a coma for several months. She dutifully stayed by his bedside day after day, tending to his every need, even shaving his face, brushing his teeth, and dealing with his Depends.

One day he opened his eyes and saw her bending over him, her eyes smiling encouragingly into his. When he started speaking his voice was so low she had to lean down closer to his lips to make out what he was saying:

"You've been with me through so many bad times," he told her. "Even back in college, when I broke my leg playing football, you rode in the ambulance with me to the hospital. When we got married and I tried and tried and tried to find a job but no one would hire me, you were there to support me. When that Mack truck hit us broadside on the freeway, you were there by my side. When we lost our home, you stood beside me on the front lawn and watched the sheriff auction off our things. And now my health is failing, and you're still here."

The woman felt tender tears welling up in her eyes as she listened to her husband recite the difficulties they had been through together.

"You know what, Agnes?" he said.

"What, dear?" she answered.

"I think you're bad luck."[1]

When I heard that story, I thought, *Now, isn't that just like a man to put that kind of spin on the story?* Although Bill was a wonderful husband and never accused me of being bad luck as we endured one calamity and crisis after another during our years together, he *did* have a way of seeing things in a pessimistic light. In fact, I used to tease him about being my favorite joy robber. For example, once when we were enjoying a rare clear day in Southern California, with the smog gone and the air crystal clear, I exclaimed, "Oh, Bill, isn't it beautiful! It looks like God has vacuumed the sky."

"Yeah," he groused, "but He'll probably dump the sweeper bag tomorrow."

"My fat has been with me through good times and bad, it stuck by me when all of my friends turned away. How dare you ask me to go on a diet?"

Finding the Dark Cloud inside the Silver Lining

There are thousands—maybe millions—of joy robbers out there, and because of Bill, I always assumed most of them were men. But I love the story about the grandmother who was walking along the seashore with her little grandson. Suddenly a monstrous wave appeared out of nowhere and swept the boy out to sea. The grandmother, horrified, fell to her knees in the sand and prayed, "God, please return my beloved grandson. Please, I beg of You. Send him back safely."

Suddenly another huge wave came rolling in and deposited the little boy on the sand at her feet. She picked him up and looked him over, then she looked up at the sky and said, "He had a hat!"[2]

"We made good time. We're already in the valley of the shadow of death."

Yes, some people have a hard time finding the joy in the minor events *and* the miracles of life.

Differing Opinions on What's Delightful

We all have a different perspective on life, but it seems to me that the older we get the more pronounced those differences are between the sexes, and especially between husbands and wives. You'd think the longer we live together the more similarities we'd develop. But for a lot of couples that's not what happens, especially in things involving technology. It always seems like one spouse is continually marching off into the world of tomorrow while the other is happily planted back in the dark ages. Since I've already told you how I clung to my old typewriters when the rest of the world moved on to computers, you won't be surprised to hear that Bill, the former navy pilot, was the high-tech member of our household.

Nothing demonstrated this high-tech, low-tech difference more vividly than the surprise Bill bought for me while I was in the hospital having brain surgery: a new space-age washer and dryer. On the day I came home from the hospital, my family led me into the laundry room for the unveiling, and there stood Bill, waiting beside the two glistening white machines topped with elaborate, computerized control panels. I felt like I'd stepped into the space shuttle cockpit.

"Ohhhh," I said, desperately wanting to run my hand nervously over my head—but encountering the staples and sutures that held my scalp together instead. "Th-that's nice. How do they work?"

"That's what the video's for," Bill said, beaming like a proud papa and pointing to a black plastic cassette. "You watch the video, and it tells you how to run 'em."

"I have to *watch a video* to learn how to do the laundry?" I moaned.

During nearly two weeks of my hospital stay, despite brain surgery and having a barbed-wire fence implanted in my scalp, I hadn't felt one moment of pain. Now a headache threatened to rumble up from somewhere near my spleen. "B-but, where are my *old* washer and dryer?"

"Oh, they hauled 'em off when they brought the new ones," Bill said with a dismissive wave of his hand.

**"I'd trade it in if it weren't for
all the socks still unaccounted for."**

©2007. Reprinted courtesy of Bunny Hoest and Parade magazine.

"You hauled them off?" I could hear my voice shifting into whining mode again. "But, Bill, I *liked* my old washer and dryer. I sure don't feel up to watching a video to learn how to wash my clothes."

"Well, you don't have to watch it *now*," he said a little huffily. "I'll do the laundry until you get back on your feet again. You're not gonna be doing *any* housework for a while."

Amazingly, my headache suddenly vanished.

And *that* incident demonstrates how you can put a positive spin on a negative incident. I hated the new washer and dryer (that was the negative part), so, forever after that, Bill did the laundry. (It just doesn't get any more positive than that!)

Driving Each Other Crazy

Another common conflict between couples as they age is their different driving styles. To put it bluntly, some of us husbands and wives drive each other crazy with our driving!

It got to be so stressful for Bill and me to ride with each other that we tried to avoid driving anywhere together at all! In my Ford Crown Victoria, I was as happy as a lark, heading off somewhere by myself to spread my joy. And Bill had a cute little sports car for running his daily errands. He had driven an ancient Volvo off and on for ages, but the year before he died, he finally gave away the twenty-four-year-old car for the last time. (We had given it away twice before, but like the dog in *Lassie, Come Home,* it kept coming back to us.)

So usually, when we were driving, we were by ourselves. That was best for both of us, because we had no backseat driver to contend with, no one ready to point out our little quirks and errors. But sometimes, even when we thought no one was looking, evidence of our occasional driving snafus leaked out. One day, after Bill had been playing pool with his friends at the recreation hall in our mobile-home park, he came home and walked into my office with a disgusted look on his face.

"What's the matter?" I asked.

"Your name is posted three times on the neighborhood complaint board!" he fumed.

"What do you mean?" I asked. "I haven't done anything wrong."

"It's posted three times under the 'speeders' sign, right there for everyone to see," he said, shaking his head. "The guys were giving me a hard time about being married to a speed demon."

Here was the former fighter pilot calling *me* a speed demon! I used to tell my girlfriends that when I rode with Bill I didn't need a seat belt because he drove so fast the centrifugal force held me securely in my seat.

"Well, how fast did the complaint board say I was going?" I asked, still amazed.

"Twenty-five in a fifteen," he answered glumly.

"Twenty-five miles an hour is *speeding*?" I argued. "Who on earth goes *fifteen* miles an hour? *No one* drives fifteen miles an hour unless they're stopped!"

Then curiosity got the best of me. "Who else's name is on the board?" I asked.

"That's the worst part," Bill replied morosely. "The list just says, 'Barbara Johnson, Barbara Johnson, Barbara Johnson.' Apparently you're the only speeder in the whole park!"

I burst out laughing. It made my day to think of myself as a seventy-something chemo-induced speeder, *tearing* around the mobile-home park at twenty-five miles an hour! And I knew immediately which of my feisty friends had posted my name—I'm sure to give me something to laugh about. (But I did try to slow down a little after that, holding my cruising speed to no more than a blazing nineteen miles per hour in the neighborhood—or at least when I was driving by her house!)

These memories are a great comfort to me now, three years after Bill died. I'm so thankful for the support he provided, the love he shared, and the laughter he induced (sometimes without meaning to). Now on my own, I look back and see that a good marriage is both a blessing and a hardship. It is a gift that brings companionship, tenderness, joy, laughter, and solace during the hard times. But it is a hard thing too, because when a good marriage ends and a widow or widower is left alone, the heartache and loss can be overwhelming.

I've sometimes thought that if Bill and I had had a mediocre marriage—if we had shared tolerance and comfort, legalities and finances, instead of love and laughter, admiration and respect—maybe these last years without him would have been easier to bear. I wouldn't miss him so much now if I hadn't loved him so much then. But what a vastly different and duller life I would have lived!

Shut Up in Precious Imprisonment

Lynda has always loved to read, and even though she has retired now from her bookstore job, she still reads "volumes of volumes," as I like to say. Lucky for me, she shares the highlights with me and gives wonderfully animated recitations of her favorite parts of the most memorable books.

Not too long ago she read Pamela Rosewell Moore's book *The Five Silent Years of Corrie ten Boom.* Bless her heart, Lynda had chosen to read it, thinking of me. I'm far from silent, but like Corrie, in the midst of busy and productive ministry work in my later years I've suddenly been waylaid by devastating health problems. Corrie suffered a stroke that prevented her from speaking. I developed a brain tumor.

Pamela Rosewell Moore was Corrie's assistant and companion for many years, and in her book she notes that Corrie's response to the stroke was the same as it was for all the hardships and setbacks she suffered throughout her life. Her family was incarcerated in prisons or work camps during the German occupation of the Netherlands for helping Jews and others despised by the Nazis. Corrie's parents and sister died during that imprisonment. Corrie survived, and she spent the rest of her life praising God and seeking to lead others to Him.

Pamela Moore remembers that Corrie's abiding philosophy had always been that it's not what happens to us that's important "but how we take it." And while the question *Why?* swirled constantly in the minds of Corrie's caretakers and visitors—Why would God let such a devastating thing happen to silence one of His most devoted servants?—Pamela noticed that it never seemed to occur to Corrie herself. "Her attitude was one of acceptance," she wrote. "God had shut her up with Himself in a kind of precious imprisonment, and so far, what was going on in her spirit was a secret between the two of them."[3]

This was the same Corrie who, as a young girl locked up in a Nazi prison, had been sent a colorful bath towel by a friend from home. To pass the time, Corrie unraveled the towel and used the thread to embroider pictures on her pajamas.

Being reminded of Corrie ten Boom's optimistic attitude and stalwart faith, I am inspired to change my own sometimes-mournful demeanor. I hope to look less often toward my losses and lean forward into the Lord's loving embrace. In my own precious imprisonment, He has given me a colorful towel of memories to dry my tears. With His help, I intend to unravel it and, with each bright thread, create a picture of joy and laughter to decorate each day I have left.

OVER THE HILL HEARTWARMERS

Say It Now
Do you want to say you love me?
Say it now, while I can hear
Your voice, soft, low, and soothing,
Gently telling me I'm dear.

Do you want to show you love me?
Hold my hand, caress my cheek,
Then just listen—only listen—
To my thoughts and hurts and dreams.

Age will change us, time will turn us,
Death will take us all too soon.
Do you want to say you love me?
Say it now. I'll say it too.

—ANN LUNA[4]

♥

I've sure gotten old! I've had two bypass surger-
ies, a hip replacement, new knees, fought breast
cancer and diabetes. I'm half blind, can't hear anything quieter than a jet engine, take forty different
medications that make me dizzy, short of breath,
and subject to blackouts. I have bouts of dementia, poor circulation, and can hardly feel my hands
and feet anymore. I can't remember if I'm eighty-
five or ninety-two, and I've lost most of my close
friends. But, thank heaven, I still have my driver's
license!

—Source Unknown

♥

Three ladies were killed in a car crash. At the
pearly gates, St. Peter informed them that there is
only one rule in heaven: don't step on the ducks.
Sure enough, the three looked around, and there
were ducks everywhere.

It wasn't long before the first woman stepped
on a duck. St. Peter came, admonished her, and
told her that her punishment was to be chained to
the ugliest man she had ever seen for all of eternity. He bound the two together and walked away.

Not too much later, the second woman stepped
on a duck and suffered the same fate.

The third woman, determined to avoid the sentence, was very careful and managed to go for many weeks without stepping on a duck. Suddenly, one day, St. Peter walked up to her and, without saying a word, chained her to a tall, dark, and handsome man. Then he walked away.

"I wonder what I did to deserve this?" the woman wondered aloud.

The man turned to her and replied, "I don't know about you . . . but I stepped on a duck!"

—SOURCE UNKNOWN

♥

"What ever happened to 'Never go to bed angry'?"

♥

Just outside the pearly gates was a line of men waiting to get in. A sign overhead read: "For Men Who Have Been Dominated By Their Wives All Their Lives." The line extended as far as the eye could see.

There was another sign nearby: "For Men Who Have Never Been Dominated By Their Wives." Only one man was standing under it.

St. Peter stepped over to him and asked, "Why are you standing here?"

The man replied, "I don't know. My wife told me to stand here."[5]

♥

Because I'm a guy, I must hold the television remote control in my hand while I watch TV. If the thing has been misplaced, I'll miss a whole show looking for it, though one time I was able to survive by holding a calculator.

—W. BRUCE CAMERON[6]

♥

You know you're getting old when everything either dries up or leaks.

♥

A man answered his doorbell and a friend walked in, followed by a very large dog. As they began talking, the dog knocked over a lamp and jumped up on the sofa with his muddy feet and began chewing on one of the pillows.

The outraged householder, unable to contain himself any longer, burst out, "Don't you think you should train your dog better?"

"*My* dog!" exclaimed the friend, surprised. "I thought it was *your* dog."[7]

♥

Happiness comes through doors you didn't even know you left open.

♥

Sign in front of a funeral home: DRIVE CAREFULLY. WE CAN WAIT.

♥

You're always young in his presence. (Psalm 103:4 MSG)

NOTES

Chapter 1. Not the Way I Planned It
1. Gene Perret, *Growing Older Is So Much Fun Everybody's Doing It* (Phoenix: Arizona Highways Book Division, 2000), 128.

Chapter 2. Finding New Purposes in Later Life
1. Mrs. George Young, quoted in Robert Morgan, *Then Sings My Soul: 150 of the World's Greatest Hymn Stories,* book 2 (Nashville: Nelson Reference, 2004). George Young wrote the hymn "God Leads Us Along" in 1903.
2. Jeremiah 29:11.
3. Martha Bolton, *Cooking with Hot Flashes* (Bloomington, MN: Bethany House, a division of Baker Publishing Group, 2004), 63.

Chapter 3. The Lovely Patina of Age
1. Ronald Reagan, quoted in James S. Denton, ed., *Grinning with the Gipper* (New York: Atlantic Monthly Press, 1988), 21.
2. Ann Luna, "Senility Hotline," © 2007. Used by permission.

Chapter 4. Celebrating Senility
1. Taken from *The Best of the Good Clean Jokes* by Bob Phillips. Copyright 1989 by Harvest House Publishers, Eugene, OR. Used by permission. www.harvesthousepublishers.com.

Chapter 5. Mothering Mayhem
1. Harland Williams, quoted in Judy Brown, *Joke Soup* (Kansas City: Andrews McMeel, 1998), 117.
2. Adapted from Streiker, *Nelson's Big Book of Laughter* (Nashville: Thomas Nelson, 2000), 159. Used by permission of Thomas Nelson, Inc.
3. Rita Rudner, quoted in Ronald L. Smith, *The Comedy Quote Dictionary* (New York: Doubleday, 1992), 99.

Chapter 6. Grow Old Along with Me.

1. Source unknown.

2. Adapted from *The Prairie Home Companion Pretty Good Joke Book,* vol. 3 (Minneapolis: Minnesota Public Radio, 1998), 3.

3. Pamela Rosewell Moore, *The Five Silent Years of Corrie ten Boom* (Grand Rapids: Zondervan, 1986), 138.

4. Ann Luna, "Say It Now," © 2007. Used by permission.

5. Adapted from Streiker, *Nelson's Big Book of Laughter* (Nashville: Thomas Nelson, 2000), 208. Used by permission of Thomas Nelson, Inc.

6. W. Bruce Cameron, www.wbrucecameron.com. Copyright © 1999. Used by permission.

7. Taken from *The Best of the Good Clean Jokes* by Bob Phillips. Copyright 1989 by Harvest House Publishers, Eugene, OR. Used by permission. www.harvesthousepublishers.com.